Exploring
Mountains

A ptarmigan.

pp

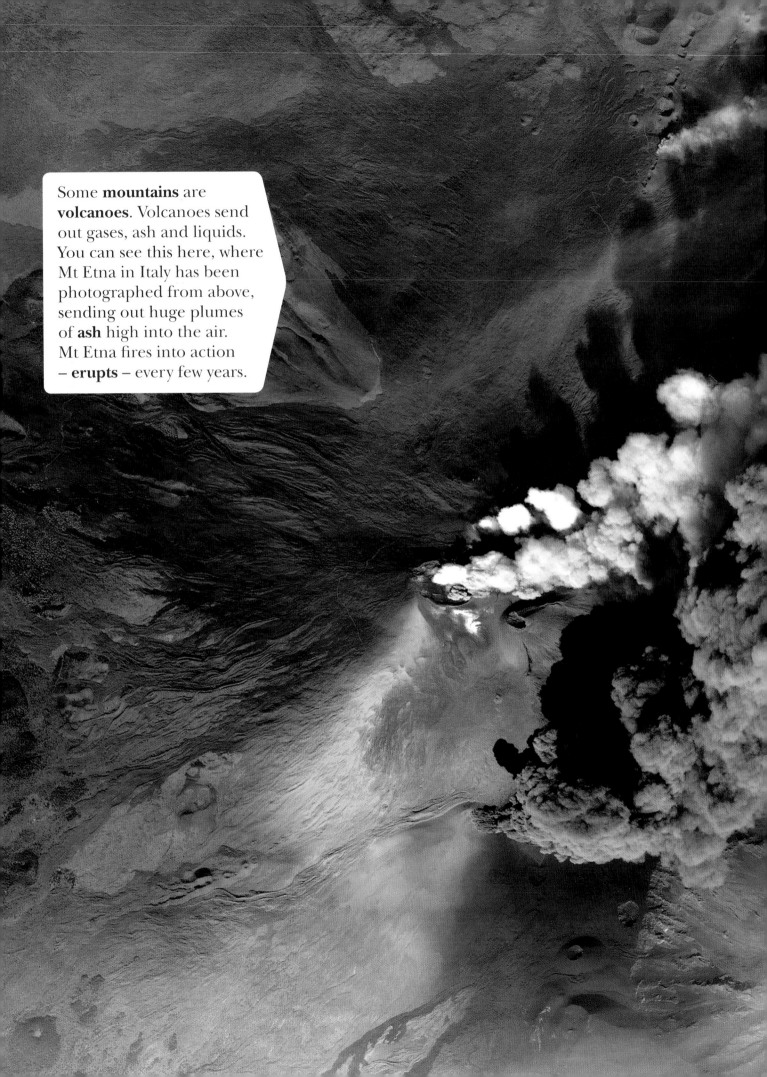

Some **mountains** are **volcanoes**. Volcanoes send out gases, ash and liquids. You can see this here, where Mt Etna in Italy has been photographed from above, sending out huge plumes of **ash** high into the air. Mt Etna fires into action – **erupts** – every few years.

Contents

Where do we find mountains? 4

Volcanoes 6

What's inside a volcano? 8

Mountain chains 10

Mountains of frost and ice 12

Mountain plants 14

Mountain animals 16

Protecting mountains 18

Mountain farming 20

Mountain passes 22

Mountain homes 24

Winter fun 26

Mountain safety 28

Try these 30

Glossary and Index 32

Look up the **bold** words in the glossary
on page 32 of this book.

Where do we find mountains?

Mountains are parts of the land that rise way above the surrounding area.

Sometimes they do this as single **peaks**. Sometimes they rise up in long lines that stretch right across the world.

Some mountains are mainly hidden because they rise up from the ocean floor. We can only see their tops.

Mountains are some of the most quickly changing parts of the Earth. Some mountains change slowly but some change very quickly. As they change they may send out towering plumes of ash and liquid rock. These make volcanoes, or they may cause **earthquakes**.

Mountains make patterns across the world. You can see these here.

Cotopaxi, Ecuador 5,897 m

Kilimanjaro, Tanzania 5,895 m

3

2

4

Mountain chains.

1
Himalayas, Asia
Mt Everest, Nepal/Tibet 8,848 m

2
Andes, South America
Aconcagua, Argentina/Chile 6,959 m

3
Rockies, North America
Mt McKinley, USA 6,194 m

| Mt Rainier, USA 4,392 m | Mauna Kea/Mauna Loa, Hawaii 4,205 m (but 9,750 m from sea floor) | Mt Fuji, Japan 3,776 m | Ruapehu, New Zealand 2,797 m | Mt St Helens, USA 2,400 m | Mt Pinatubo, Philippines 1,460 m | Mt Vesuvius, Italy 1,277 m |

Famous volcanoes.

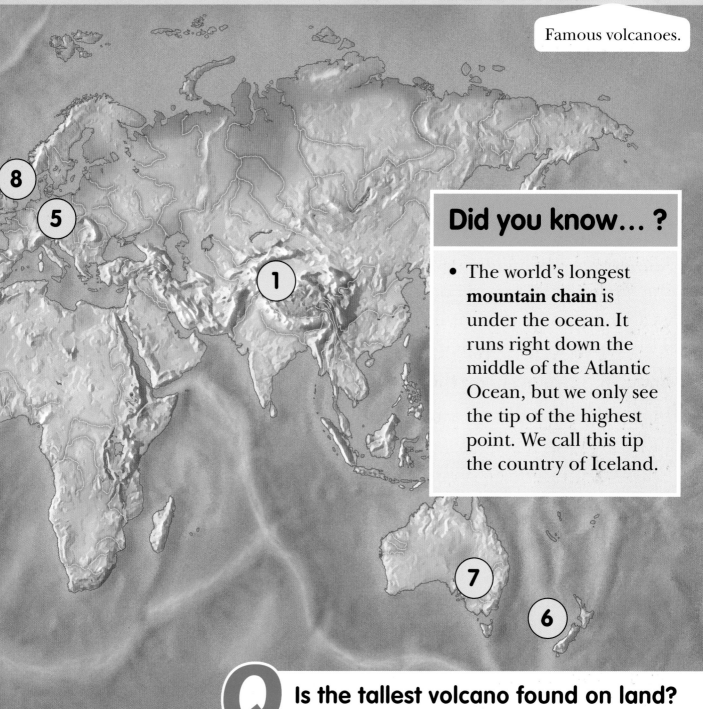

Did you know…?

- The world's longest **mountain chain** is under the ocean. It runs right down the middle of the Atlantic Ocean, but we only see the tip of the highest point. We call this tip the country of Iceland.

Q **Is the tallest volcano found on land?**

| Antartica nson Massif 4,897 m | Alps, Europe Mont Blanc, France/Italy 4,807 m | Southern Alps, New Zealand Mt Cook, New Zealand 3,765 m | Great Dividing Range, Australia Mt Kosciusko, Australia 2,230 m | United Kingdom Ben Nevis, Scotland 1,344 m Snowdon, Wales 1,085 m Scafell Pike, England 978 m Slieve Donard, Northern Ireland 850 m |

Volcanoes

Deep beneath the Earth's surface (the **crust**) the rock is so hot that it is liquid. We call liquid rock **magma**.

If there is a weakness in the Earth's crust, this magma can force its way to the surface.

Sometimes the magma gets to the surface easily and comes out as a fountain of orange liquid. This liquid rock is called **lava**.

Sometimes the way up is blocked. Then the pressure in the magma builds and builds until finally it blasts the blockage away. The magma flies out of the ground so quickly that the lava breaks up into a spray of tiny pieces. These cool almost instantly into a fine dust called **ash**.

The Hawaiian Islands erupt runny lava.

Did you know…?

- Some volcanoes open as gigantic splits along the Earth's surface. These are called fissure volcanoes. Most undersea volcanoes are of this kind.
- Lava is an orange colour when it is liquid, but as it cools it turns red and then black.
- Magma has gas dissolved in it just like gas is dissolved in a fizzy drink. If the magma comes to the surface very quickly, the gas blows the liquid apart, sending up a plume of fine particles into the air.
- Magma is of two kinds: sticky and runny. The runny kind comes to the surface as lava. The sticky kind comes to the surface as an explosion of ash.

Mt St Helens in North America exploded suddenly in 1980. It erupted sticky lava and sent a huge plume of ash and gas into the air.

What is the liquid called that comes from a volcano?

What's inside a volcano?

Volcanoes are mountains made of lava and ash. If you look inside the top of a volcano you can see the two kinds of rock making layers inside the walls.

All volcanoes are fed from huge chambers of molten rock – magma chambers – deep below the surface.

A volcano erupts when the chamber is completely full. The pressure of the liquid and gas in the chamber sends magma up a pipe (**vent**) to the surface. The volcano erupts until the chamber is empty, then the volcano quietens down until the chamber refills. This may take hundreds of years.

Did you know... ?

- A volcano is made of layers of rock.
- If you count the layers you know how many times the volcano has erupted.
- Runny lava flows like water and travels long distances.
- Sticky lava flows more like cement and only travels a little way.
- If the volcano has steep sides, the magma chamber below is full of sticky lava.
- If the volcano has gentle sides, the magma chamber below is full of runny lava.

This picture looks down at lava (orange) inside the top, or **crater**, of a volcano. The white bands in the crater walls are rock made of ash. The dark bands are rock made of lava.

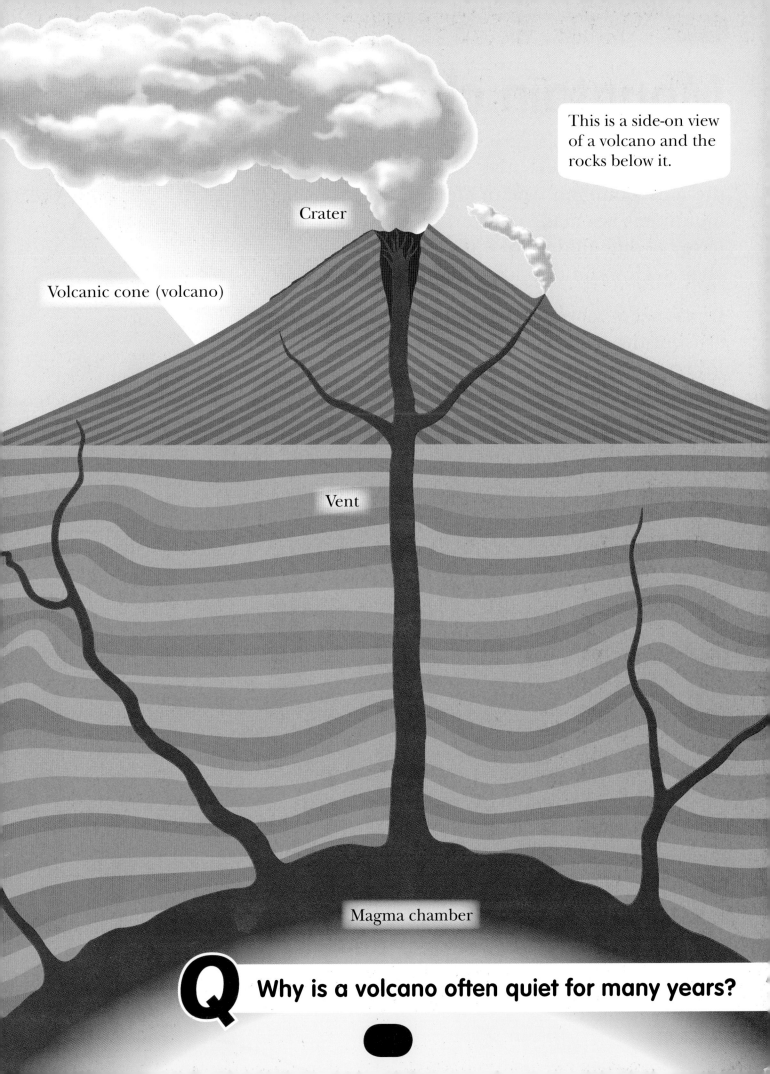

This is a side-on view of a volcano and the rocks below it.

Crater

Volcanic cone (volcano)

Vent

Magma chamber

Q **Why is a volcano often quiet for many years?**

Mountain chains

Volcanoes are spectacular, but they are not the most common type of mountain. Most mountains are made of layers of rock that have become folded up into long curving chains. How did this come about?

It may seem incredible, but the 'solid' crust of the Earth is actually quite thin. Like the thickness of its skin is to an apple. Underneath the crust is all molten rock.

The molten rock moves slowly about. It drags the crust with it.

This splits the crust in some places and lava flows out. (We don't often see this because it usually happens under the oceans.)

In other places it pushes the crust together, folding it up into huge mountain chains.

Each fold in a chain is called a **mountain range**. The Himalaya are part of the land mountain chain with the tallest peaks.

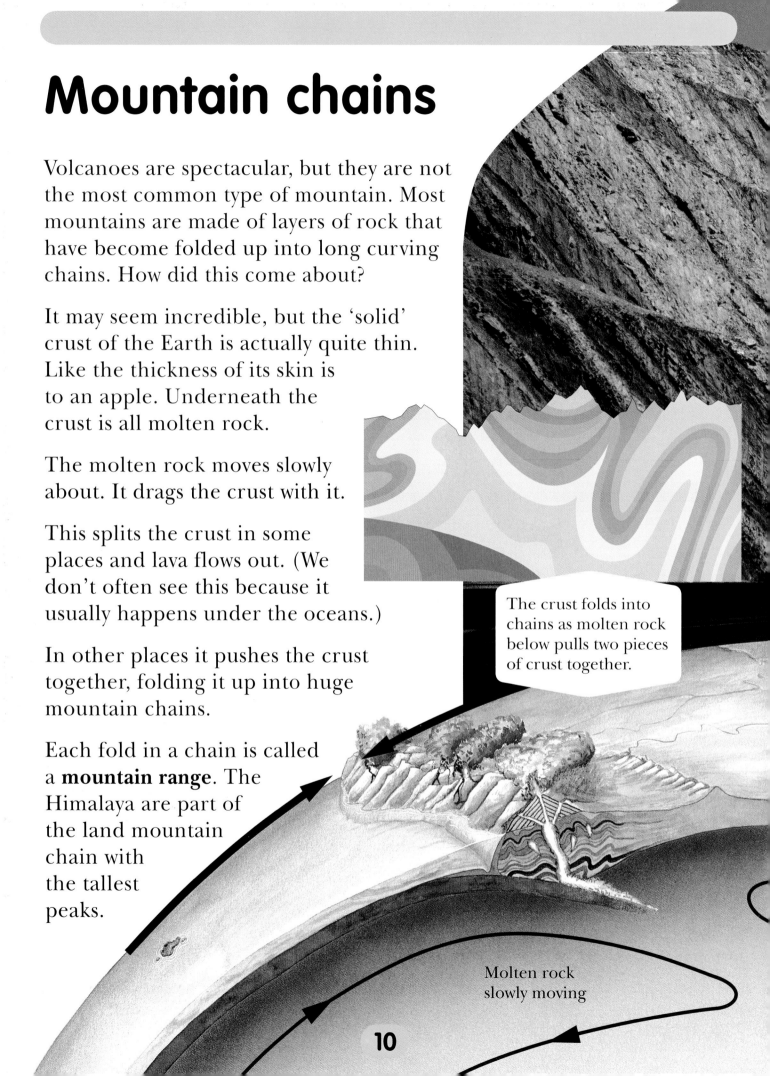

The crust folds into chains as molten rock below pulls two pieces of crust together.

Molten rock slowly moving

- That the rocks deep in the crust are hot and can fold quite easily.
- That the Earth's surface rocks are hard. They do not fold easily and so tend to crack and slide over one another.
- Every time an earthquake occurs it is a sign that a mountain chain is folding up a bit more, and the surface rocks are cracking up.

Here is an exaggerated view of the places where the crust splits, as molten rock below pulls in two directions. You can see it is mostly in the oceans.

Sometimes you can see the folded rocks in mountains, for example, where there is a deep road cutting.

Can you find a place where earthquakes are quite frequent?

Mountains of frost and ice

Mountain peaks stand high above the rest of the land. The air at the top is cold, and in winter snow falls.

For month after month the snow piles up on the ground, and the snow is crushed to ice. Summers are short and not all of the ice melts, so that more ice is added each winter. The ice fills mountain hollows and valleys, forming rivers of ice called **glaciers**.

The glaciers slowly slide down valleys under their own enormous weight.

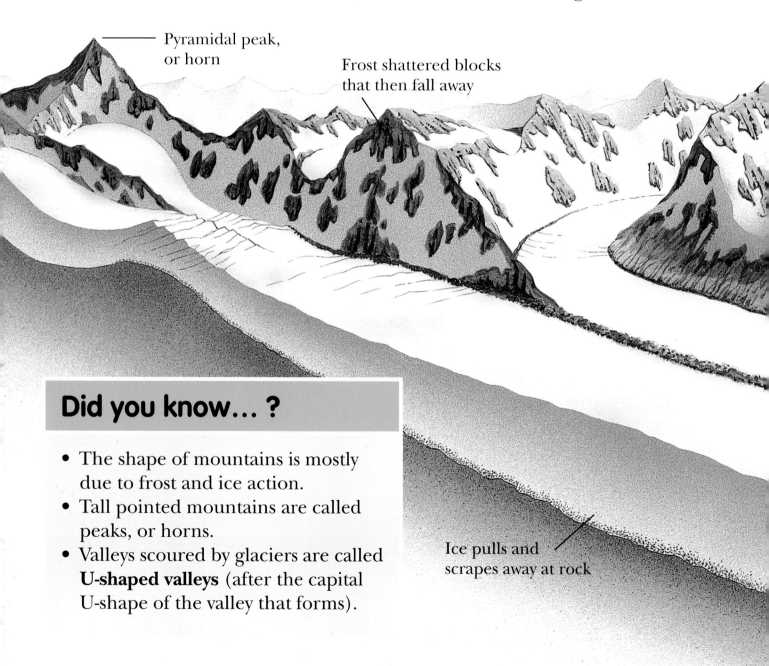

Pyramidal peak, or horn

Frost shattered blocks that then fall away

Ice pulls and scrapes away at rock

Did you know... ?

- The shape of mountains is mostly due to frost and ice action.
- Tall pointed mountains are called peaks, or horns.
- Valleys scoured by glaciers are called **U-shaped valleys** (after the capital U-shape of the valley that forms).

The ice also drags against the valley floor, pulling out pieces of rock. These sharp rocky fragments are then scraped across the valley floor, grinding yet more rock away.

On the mountainsides it is too steep for ice to build up and the rocks stay bare. These bare rocks are attacked by frost. The frost loosens pieces of rock, which then fall onto the glaciers below.

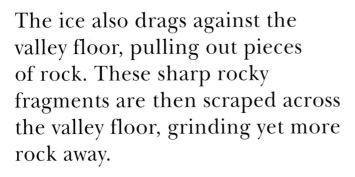

Glacier

In some mountain areas we see U-shaped valleys clearly because the glaciers have melted away. These diagrams show you how the valleys formed.

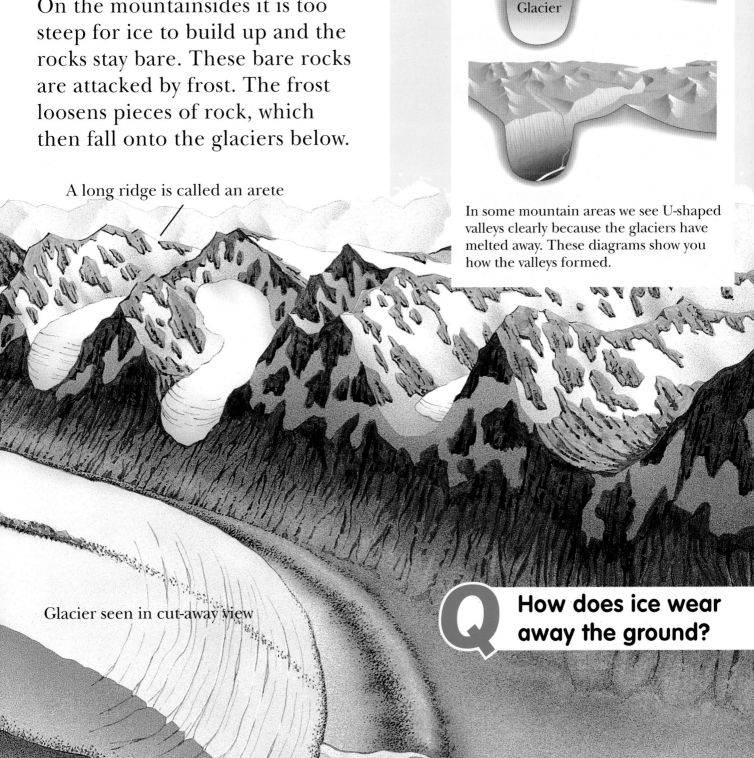

A long ridge is called an arete

Glacier seen in cut-away view

Q How does ice wear away the ground?

Alpine snowbells blooming as soon as the snow melts in June.

Few, if any plants can grow on the bare rocky cliffs at mountain tops.

Meadows

Conifer trees, such as pine, firs and spruce grow up to the tree line. They may also be mixed with some hardy broadleaved trees, such as birch and aspen.

Tree line. The upper limit where a forest can grow.

The edge of the forest and the start of the meadowland.

Broadleaved trees, such as oak, grow on the lowest slopes.

Mountain plants

It is much colder, snowier and windier at the top of a mountain than down in a nearby valley. As a result, there are many kinds of plants on a mountain, as you can see here.

The best time to see mountain flowers is in early June.

 What are alpine plants?

Mountain animals

Golden eagle

Raven

There is not much food on a mountain, so there are few animals.

Many animals only visit the mountains in summer, when the snow has melted away. In autumn they move down to nearby valleys where the weather is less harsh.

Those that stay in the mountains may find deep burrows in the ground, or seek the shelter of caves. They then mainly sleep (hibernate) until the spring.

A few stay active all winter. Many of them change colour, from brown in summer to white in winter.

Bears eat both plants and animals. They move to valleys in the winter, looking for a den to hibernate in during the coldest part of the year.

It is common for mountain animals to change their colour with the seasons to give themselves camouflage. In summer, hares are patterned brown. They turn white in winter.

This is an Apollo butterfly. Only a few butterflies can survive the cool summers.

Mountain goats are skilled climbers and can climb near-vertical cliffs.

Red deer graze on mountain pastures only in summer.

Lynx – a fearsome mountain hunter.

Ptarmigan are grouse-like birds that scratch down through the snow to browse on plants. They also burrow under the snow to protect themselves from the weather overnight.

Marmot, a rodent. Many small mountain animals live in a network of tunnels in the bouldery soil which they can use to hibernate in winter.

Q **Why do some animals change colour in winter?**

The dipper is adapted to fast flowing mountain streams, but is a summer visitor only.

Protecting mountains

Many people visit mountains. More than 30 million people go on holiday to the Alps alone! Many of them who go walking, on coach tours, or skiing, do not realise how fragile the land is. People pollute the air and make it hard for plants to grow. They trample all over mountains and leave litter. They want ski resorts near all of the mountains. They also want to watch the wildlife, but it is hard for wild animals to live with so many people about. Many mountain animals are now endangered. They can be saved only if some land is set aside for wilderness and national parks.

Skiing holidays bring tens of millions of people to mountain areas in winter.

Tourists clog up mountain villages and buy up houses, so the towns become full of holiday homes.

Why do people visit mountain areas?

Mountain farming

Mountains are hard places to farm. The weather is very cold and it is snowy in winter and often wet in summer. Even grass grows slowly and no crops can be grown at all. This is why most mountain farmers rear animals.

To make the best of the short growing season, farmers send their animals to high mountain pastures as soon as the snows have melted. Then they let the grass in the valley grow, harvest it and store it in barns.

As the first snows fall, the animals are brought back to the valleys, kept in the barns and fed on the hay that was collected earlier in the year.

It is a hard life and mountain farmers do not make much money.

In the summer all the family work hard on the field in the valley, helping to gather in the hay.

During the summer, cattle and goats are allowed to roam free. In the Alps, the animals all have bells around their necks.

In the winter, cows are kept in barns.

Q Why are animals kept in barns during the winter?

Mountain passes

It is difficult to travel through the mountains because of the steep slopes and bad weather.

Many roads have large numbers of hairpin bends or switchbacks. Most railways have to use tunnels to get between valleys.

Much of Switzerland is in the Alps. If you travel on their motorways you are always passing over huge bridges and then diving into long tunnels. These roads are very expensive to build.

Trains can only get between valleys if long tunnels are dug through the mountains.

Here you can see a road making its way down one valley side and up the other.

Did you know… ?

- The highest **pass** with a proper road is called Semo La. It is 5,575 m high and is in the Himalaya of Tibet.
- The highest pass in the Andes is Chacaltaya at 5,100 m. It is in Bolivia.
- The highest pass in North America is in the Rocky Mountains National Park. It rises to 3,713 m.
- Passes interest so many people that some are well known even though few people visit them. For example, the Great St Bernard Pass (2,473 m) in the Alps.
- Many quite low passes have been the sites of famous battles, for example the Khyber Pass (1,027 m) between Afghanistan and Pakistan.

Many people visit mountains in summer for the spectacular views. They do not mind travelling slowly.

Q **Why do the roads have hairpin bends?**

Mountain homes

People have lived in the mountains for thousands of years. To protect themselves from the cold and wind of winter, and the deep snow, they have built special homes.

Here you can see a side view of a traditional wooden farmhouse. Animals are at the bottom, people live in the middle and front, and hay is stored in the back and in part of the roof. Wood is cut in summer and piled against the walls so it is easy to reach and burn as fuel in winter.

This is what mountain homes look like in winter. Many are buried in snow almost up to their roofs!

Here is an old Alpine mountain home in summer. The walls are very thick and the windows small in order to keep out the cold. The slit windows at the bottom let light in to the place where the animals are kept in winter (a byre). Snow is so deep it comes well up the walls during the winter months.

Q Why are there steps up to the house?

Winter fun

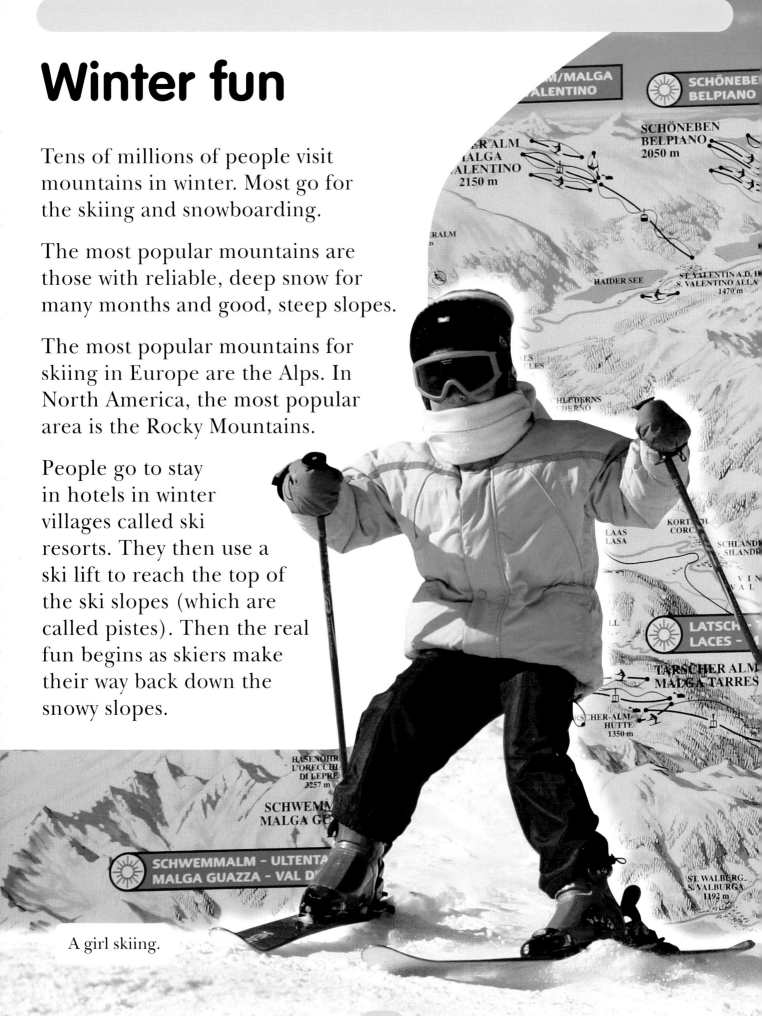

Tens of millions of people visit mountains in winter. Most go for the skiing and snowboarding.

The most popular mountains are those with reliable, deep snow for many months and good, steep slopes.

The most popular mountains for skiing in Europe are the Alps. In North America, the most popular area is the Rocky Mountains.

People go to stay in hotels in winter villages called ski resorts. They then use a ski lift to reach the top of the ski slopes (which are called pistes). Then the real fun begins as skiers make their way back down the snowy slopes.

A girl skiing.

Some people ski across the tops of the mountains.

This is a part of the Alps showing the ski routes, or pistes. See how many there are!

Q **What special clothes do you need?**

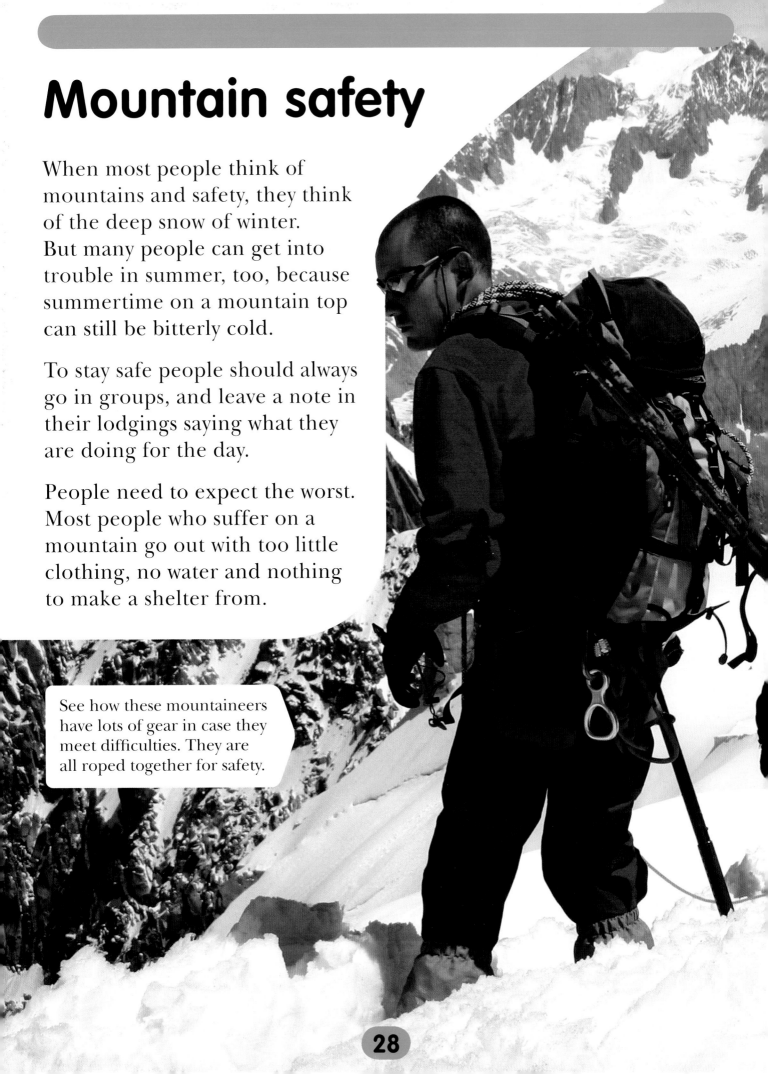

Mountain safety

When most people think of mountains and safety, they think of the deep snow of winter. But many people can get into trouble in summer, too, because summertime on a mountain top can still be bitterly cold.

To stay safe people should always go in groups, and leave a note in their lodgings saying what they are doing for the day.

People need to expect the worst. Most people who suffer on a mountain go out with too little clothing, no water and nothing to make a shelter from.

See how these mountaineers have lots of gear in case they meet difficulties. They are all roped together for safety.

As snow settles on steep slopes, its weight makes it more and more likely to slip. Once it begins slipping, millions of tonnes of snow can move at the speed of an express train. This is an **avalanche**. It is not wise to ski or to build houses in places where avalanches are common.

Q **Why do we need mountain rescue teams?**

Try these...

Make an ice cube glacier

- Put some sand (the sort builders call sharp sand) into the bottom of a small plastic (slightly flexible) bowl.
- Add water nearly to the top.
- Put the bowl in the freezer and wait for a day.
- Push the glacier out of the bowl.
- Look at the bottom of the glacier. Rub your hand over it.
- Rub the glacier on to an old sheet of plastic. First rub with the top (sand-free) surface. Then turn it over and rub with the sandy surface. See what the difference is.

Make a mountain chain

- You can see how fold mountains are formed by using a tablecloth spread out on a table.
- You need at least four people, two on one side of the table and two on the other. Fold mountains form when slabs of the Earth's crust (modelled by the tablecloth) push together.
- The picture shows how to make the mountains. Try to model the shape of the Himalaya and the Alps (see an atlas to find out their shapes). When you get the shape right you will know how the Earth's crust moved!

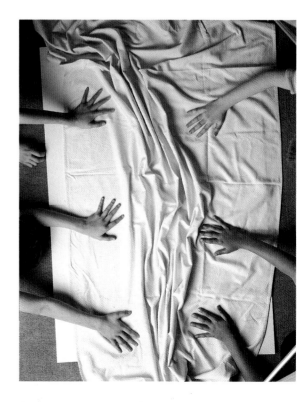

A world of activities

How many different ways can you see the mountain landscape being used? Write them down to see who gets the longest list.

Glossary

ash Fine sandy and dusty material that is thrown out of an erupting volcano.

avalanche A fast-moving mass of snow.

crater The depression at the top of a volcano.

crust The solid rock that surrounds the Earth.

earthquake Shaking of the ground when a part of the Earth's crust moves.

erupt To throw out violently.

glacier A mass of ice flowing down a valley.

lava Liquid rock that comes out of a volcano.

magma Liquid rock below the Earth's surface.

mountain A part of the Earth's surface that rises sharply to great height above its surroundings.

mountain chain A very large area of mountains, stretching in a line for thousands of kilometres.

mountain range A line of mountains which is usually part of a mountain chain.

pass A low gap in a mountain range.

peak A mountain summit surrounded with sharp sides.

U-shaped valley A valley carved by a glacier and which has very steep sides and a nearly flat bottom. When looking up such a valley its shape can look like a capital U.

vent The pipe or fissure through which lava and ash are erupted.

volcano A mountain which erupts lava and ash.

Index

alpine plants **15**
Alps **5, 22, 26**
Andes **4, 23**
animals **16**
ash **2, 4, 6, 7, 8**
avalanche **29**

crater **8, 9**
crust **6, 10, 11**

earthquake **4, 11**
erupt **2**
explode **7**

farming **20**
frost **12, 13**

glacier **12, 13, 30**

hairpin bends **22**

Hawaii **6**
hibernate **16**
Himalaya **4, 23**

ice **12**

lava **6, 7, 8, 10**

magma **6**
magma chamber **8, 9**
meadow **14**
mountain chain **10, 30**
mountain range **10**
mountain safety **28**

pass **22, 23**
pasture **20**
peak **4, 12**

plants **14, 15**
pollute **18**

Rockies **4, 23, 26**

ski resort **18**
skiing **26, 27**
snow **12**
snowboarding **26**
Switzerland **22**

train **22**
tree line **14**
tunnel **22, 23**

U-shaped valley **12, 13**

vent **8**
volcano **2, 4, 5, 6, 7, 8, 9**

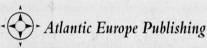

Curriculum Visions

Curriculum Visions is a registered trademark of Atlantic Europe Publishing Company Ltd.

-◈- **Atlantic Europe Publishing**

Curriculum Visions Explorers
This series provides straightforward introductions to key worlds and ideas.

You might also be interested in
Our slightly more detailed book, 'The Mountain Book'. There is a Teacher's Guide to match 'The Mountain Book'. Additional notes in PDF format are also available from the publisher to support 'Exploring mountains'. All of these products are suitable for KS2.

Dedicated Web Site
Watch movies, see many more pictures and read much more in detail about mountain environments at:

www.curriculumvisions.com
(Professional Zone: subscription required)

First published in 2007 by Atlantic Europe Publishing Company Ltd
Copyright © 2007 Earthscape

Author
Brian Knapp, BSc, PhD

Educational Consultants
JM Smith (former Deputy Head of Wellfield School, Burnley, Lancashire); the Librarians of Hertfordshire School Library Service

Senior Designer
Adele Humphries, BA

Editor
Gillian Gatehouse

Photographs
The Earthscape Picture Library, except ShutterStock p1, 16 (bear), 26, 29 (inset), 30 (glacier); USGS p2–3, 6–7 and 8 (Griggs J.D.); 7 (Austin Post).

Illustrations
David Woodroffe except p4–5 *Julian Baker* and p31 *Nicolas Debon*

Designed and produced by
Earthscape

Printed in China by
WKT Company Ltd

**Exploring mountains
– *Curriculum Visions***
A CIP record for this book is available from the British Library
ISBN 978 1 86214 208 4

This product is manufactured from sustainable managed forests. For every tree cut down at least one more is planted.